only 1 her

only 1 her

a.g.

Published by Tablo

interlude

This is for the ones who never got the apology for loving too
hard
For the ones who were called crazy for their intuition being right
For the ones with discernment stronger than the ocean waves
crashing
For the ones with a heart so forgiving as our God
For the ones full of wounds and scars
For the ones who tried to understand the person who hurt them
and their reasons why
For the ones who tried to fix what they didn't even break
For the ones who seek peace in the chaos of their mind
For the ones who pray for their healing every single night

I know your pain
I know your cries
I know your thoughts
I know it's not in you to do them the same
I know it's not in you to seek revenge for everything they've
done
I know you don't regret the love you gave
I know if you had the choice you wouldn't even want them to
know the taste
I know you're bigger than that

I'm sorry you were unappreciated and undervalued
I'm sorry your worth was never recognized
I'm sorry your heart was not in good hands
I'm sorry you were left when things got hard between you two
I'm sorry your voice was always silenced
I'm sorry your love was never reciprocated

I'm sorry you were made to seem as somebody you're not for all
the evidence you had
I'm sorry you were made to seem as if you did all the bad
I'm sorry you lost yourself trying to understand why
I'm sorry you forgot who you were when you looked in the
mirror

Please never allow another to make you feel that way
Please allow yourself to heal
Please never stop loving
Please never stop growing
Please don't ever settle again

you are worth more than you know
you are a reflection of the sun
you are 1 of 1
One that is made so unique

I hold space for you
I root for you
I stand for you
I will continue to speak for you

I'm sorry you never got your apology
I'm sorry you never got your closure
But I pray you allow this letter to open the door to your healing

ysbh

for those who are no longer here

who have left
or that i had to walk away from
or that are in heaven

i am still rooting for you
i still pray for you
i still love you

i wish you could experience this birth with me
i know you'd be proud

thank you for all the lessons that turned into wisdom
you were a chapter in my story of life

may you find peace along your journey
it's still love on this side

like kehlani said, you should be here.

sometimes no closure, is closure.

-don't touch the door

the ones who birthed me
who were supposed to love me most
who were supposed to nurture me
left me
so what makes you think i need you?

-why would i beg anybody to stay in my life?

fake love

you left me in the dark

now that i've blossomed
you reach out to me?

daddy's little angel

i'm waving my hands
my face and body are nearly six feet under

you couldn't hear my cries
or gasps for air

but you still saw me

what do you mean you didn't know?
i can see that you see me drowning

if you see then you know

i'm crying out to the heavenly father above
i'm crying out to the "father" i have on earth

i can't get out of this ocean
you're the anchor

i kinda just accept things for what they are.
what i can't change, i leave to my God.

we lost ourselves
trying to find love in each other

i was so deep in you
you were so deep in me

wall masks

i know you
i know you like no other
more than you know you

so why're you acting like you don't know that?

-why front?

last place

i know you told me you want to be alone
and seek the waters

so when the water gets too deep
when the sun sets and it gets dark
when the wind becomes too cold

i pray the footsteps
along the shoreline i left for you
when you started to swim
will guide you back home

sight

i have dreams of you
of us
i don't ever wanna wake up

i have visions of you
of us

and i wish you were the real you again
so you can see the bigger picture
our picture
the picture we created

sorry mother

it's not me
it's you

your foul energy
your ungodly soul
does not match my happiness

you are part of who i used to be
but today no more

i shall wash you off
exfoliate the trauma
and rinse it down the drain

i pray for your healing

hosea 6:1

god says he can mend, heal, fix, and bring back to life
what we think died

so do you think he can revive us?

intertwined soul ties

i hear you without you having to speak
i feel you without you having to spill
i know you without you having to front

-i still feel your soul's spirit everywhere i go.

alive

i'm finding myself again
i'm healing
i'm loving myself more
i'm breathing more
i'm living more
i'm getting closer to God

i'm restoring the holes from the roots
that you ripped out of me
when you left with your love

love from a distance

i prefer my own company

my solitude is everything

respect my space
respect my silence
respect my distance
respect my no reply
respect my healing process
respect my days off
respect my bad days
respect my peace

know your boundaries

-please understand i don't owe
anybody an explanation.
my boundaries are not for you,
and they are not meant to
make you comfortable.

unapologetically me

i stopped apologizing
i started speaking firmly
i now speak with confidence

never will i dim my light
just to make somebody else feel comfortable

-that's called insecurities.

1 corinthians 13:4-8

i know that if one doesn't love God the way i love Him
or love others the way God does
they wouldn't be able to love me properly

*-if it ain't a reflection of what God
says love is, i don't want it!*

pet peeve

i wish society would stop portraying growth and healing
as an aesthetic post cause in reality it's not.
it's the very thing us humans try to avoid
without even noticing or trying at least once in their life.
it hurts, really bad.
and i'm not gonna sit here and try to make it sound softer.
it's extremely uncomfortable.
it will have you lost, confused, anxious, depressed,
below rock bottom, triggered and sometimes hopeless.
it's not just bubble baths, self care, face masks and candles.
it's getting up when you don't feel like it,
it's leaving your comfort zone,
leaving the only things you may ever know of,
cutting certain people off,
unlearning some things to learn the right things.
don't get me wrong, at the end it's really a beautiful journey
and i'm not saying to hate it or despise it.
i'm just tired of it being tossed around so loosely.

-you ever had to re open your wounds
*you **thought** were healed just to **fully** heal?*

quiet

strength and peace is when you no longer care about other people knowing your side of the story.

ONLY 1 HER

pure, holy, divine, the truth
a God fearing woman
her love
her touch
her energy
her soul
her heart
her mind
her voice
her body
her laughs
her femininity
her beliefs
her strengths
her impact
her legacy
her loyalty
her knowledge
her worship
her roots
her growth
her testimonies
her story
i am her
there is only 1 of me

-and you will only get to fully experience me once.

the irony

too many words not enough action
too many apologies not enough change
too many wrongs too much forgiveness

-love can be such a contradiction

3

notice who's always silent. notice who always has something negative to say every time you tell them your vision or tell them about something good that God did for you.

szns

the dark season that you're in isn't permanent

after winter is spring
after spring is summer
after summer is fall

*-change is inevitable so you might as well embrace every moment
and lesson in each season.*

prayers

they keep saying i'll see better days soon but i don't know when

i tell myself to stop writing about you
but my mind continues to bleed

God is the only one who can save me
would you have let him take me?

i'm exhausted
mentally
spiritually
physically

i'm praying every day and night to heal my pain

this shit isn't for the aesthetics
you'll never get it

i had to replace my addiction of you with this journal
so instead of calling you up this would be the closest i'll get to it

my heart has sunken deeper into my stomach
the deeper i go onto the surface of this paper with this pen

they keep saying i'll see better days soon but i don't know when

so i keep my faith too and i keep asking god, "but when is soon?"

2 corinthians 5:7

walk by crazy faith
not by sight

don't let your current situation aka what you see with your sight
determine your faith towards your vision.

matthew 14:29

what is faith?

she was in a boat barely surviving
in an ocean full of chaos

God showed up in the midst of it

he said to her, "come"

she had wavy faith

but she stood up
she stepped out of the boat

her and god both walked on water

vibes

never apologize for your aura coming off "too strong"
some can't handle it
some will get intimidated by your confidence

o.k.

it's okay to unlearn some things to learn the right things
there's nothing wrong with reprogramming

sometimes it's necessary

*-it's all a learning process
but also a beautiful journey.*

punani makes the world go round

your femininity and confidence will always intimidate
fragile, insecure, narcissistic, and misogynistic men

-don't retaliate, they are sick.
wish them well and continue to slay.

be still

in solitude one can feel most lonely

but in solitude is where you grow
no distractions, no outsiders
just you and God

in solitude there is empowerment

you find strength
you find yourself
your vision becomes clearer
you start loving yourself more
you realize your worth
you become aligned
you become wiser
you learn patience
it is peace
it is sacred

-do not be afraid of it,
fall in love with it.

genesis 12:1-3 /my calling

i was comfortable
i was happy
i was living

then i had to leave everything i knew
to live in a whole new world

it never made sense to me

i was alone
i was scared
i was in survival mode

i used to ask God, "why me?"
now i know why it had to be me

i was called
i was marked
it lead me to my purpose

-sometimes we may not understand why it had to happen the way it
did. we sometimes may feel like we lost it all, but it was the very thing
that causes you to soon have better. you may not see it now, but love, it
will all make sense and you will be thankful you went through that
season to receive that garden.

i gave you life without having to go half on a baby
i gave you life without having to touch you

i spoke love into your heart

i planted a home in you
with the shovel and seed you gave me

i shared wisdom through the guarded wall that i let down for
you
without saying a word

we shared God's plan together as 1

it is deeper than what the naked eye can see
it is realer than what the perishable and sinful flesh can feel

use your soul's spirit to listen
because i'm where it wants to be

views

nowadays.. things are different
the air is different
the season is different
i think different
i speak different
my goals are different
my circle is different
my views are different
my vision is different
topic of conversations are different

life is different when you wake up
aligned to your inner self and purpose

nowadays.. we may not relate anymore
and i'm okay with that

lost and found

we kept living life trying to find each other in others
but we couldn't

you told me we were each other's puzzle piece

we still are

rebirth

her tears were the rain
that watered her own seeds
under concrete

little did she know each tear drop
represented a new home
of self love
happiness
clarity
healing

little did she know
her tears from the pain would grow her
into a collection of roses and daisies

little did she know
the garden she grew
would be her heaven on earth

i just want to know how you're doing

i know we set out to grow more
but i'm growing anxious

i'm dying to hear your voice
to feel your lips
to feel your hands
to feel your love

i don't want to know about anybody else
i don't want to know your experience
i don't want to know if you gave another
your time, affection, energy, and presence

cause then i'll know you had intentions of moving on
cause then i'll know you were still seeking the waters
while i was seeking to be the best woman i could be
here at home
for you
for us
for me

-it hasn't been too long though it feels like forever.
i want to know how you're doing, but sometimes
some things are better left unsaid.

shame, less? mind, less?

i'm told it's not my fault
i'm told to distance myself
i tell myself, "you don't need that in your life"
i don't

but what is a daughter without a father?
i guess you can now say, a woman
an independent one

the drastic changes hit
but the blessings that hit compare to none

your caller id says your name but is that really you?

is your mind over the clouds watching the new you take over?

psalms and songs

i guess i held onto our psalms

it was our words of our love story
that were written and spoken
that never allowed me to let go

the blue print was there

our psalms consisted of endurance
divinity
faith
past eternal love
truth
promises

our psalms were my favorite songs
that i never wanted to stop playing

the heavens put their stamp on it

God created it
we walked it
we lived it

lightyears

my heart
soul
mind
i feel like i was born in another life

i'm an old soul in a new body

or maybe i was meant to be this grown at such a young age?

luv 2 luv

you know that love where you just admire your significant other
while their driving?

where that admiration turns into realization
that this is your person?

i adore that love.

antioch, ca   8:40PM   my bed

our vibe and connection so strong
we don't even need to say a word

our exchange of energy
is as destructive and powerful as a nuclear bomb

your eyes
the stars i can count
the constellation i see in them
i look into them and know we're meant

as we hold hands and smile in silence
i can read your mind
i'm pretty sure you can read mine too

don't speak, love
let our passion take over

-i know i'm not crazy
but i want this forever.

the letter// kehlani

dear mom,

sometimes i wish you never left me. sometimes i wish you
wanted to work things out. sometimes i wish you would
somehow find my number and call me for lunch to see how i'm
doing. sometimes i wish i knew what it's like to be held by you.
sometimes i wish i knew a mother's unconditional love.
sometimes i wish you loved me so that i wouldn't be mean to
those who try to replace your love and love me. sometimes i
wish things were different between us. then i remember things
are different between us because we're too different, clearly. then
i remember not to beg for love, especially love that's supposed to
come from one who made me. then i snap out of it and remind
myself i don't want to ever be the person you are or be around
you. i remind myself that if you wanted to be in my life i
wouldn't be writing this right now.

take a look in the mirror

you want to "protect me" from bad energy
yet you are the bad energy

toxic family members

let's get rid of the norm on the obligation/entitlement to remain in contact with family members, simply because you are "blood." it's okay to cut toxic people off without feeling guilty about it. don't fall for their narcissistic and manipulative ways. for the sake of your peace and healing, do what you need to do. even if it means losing other people that are against you cutting those toxic family members off, so be it. sometime's you'll need to also cut the connected branches off a tree, too. it's not being petty, it's not because you're unhealed, or broken, it's choosing yourself and your peace over their toxicity. it's loving from a distance with no hard feelings. you did the right thing, love.

and for the people who are against you cutting off those toxic family members:

stop invalidating other people's feelings/decisions simply because you use "blood" as an excuse to enable toxic and abusive behavior. it's not you, so please put yourself in their shoes. their reason is their reason and it doesn't matter if you agree or not regardless of age. you have no right to tell one how to feel or how to go about it. when you side the abuser you become the enabler.

reminder:

you are not fake or selfish for removing yourself
from bad energy that stunts your growth
whether you've known them for years or minutes
it's okay to remove yourself peacefully
history does not define present loyalty
nor does it define permanence

-in order to fully prosper you must outgrow
certain things and certain people to discover
the new right things, and people meant for you.

my growth is not an aesthetic mood board on pinterest. bettering myself is not an aesthetic. what i put out isn't "mood" on social media. it's my life. i put out what i hope will heal others that are going through things, too. it's not a look, it's what brought me out of my old sad life.

keep it

what you give and put out is what you get back and more.

the universe is listening
God is listening

a lost orphan in the middle

when you left me
you left me lost in the dark
i had no choice but to leave
i had nowhere to go

-although i was lost, i found me– a new me.

safe haven

my safe place is being in your arms

it's like you're my bubble of sanity, peace, balance
safe zone, i'm home

you take away my hurt and worries

when i'm with you the world no longer orbits
not a thing matters but only in that moment

i wish i could live in those precious moments forever

-good thing is, you are my reality
and at least i have you.

features ft. us

your lips
so soft
so gentle

your eyes
so mesmerizing
strong enough to snatch my soul

strong enough to tell a love story
our love story

stay

i never want you to leave
i never want to leave you
i never want to see you drive off

i wish i could be at ease in your arms
boundless
timeless

every last kiss turns into one more
every last goodbye turns into one more tight hug

i miss you before you even leave me

mind yours

i'm always told to cover up
that if i show my stomach or my toothpick thighs
i will become a target
yes, i will become a target
to one who is sick and perverted
not to a human with a penis or vagina

rapists rape people, not clothes

i'm told to cover up because "i'm too young"
yes, i'm too young for the sick and perverted
who crave me

i am told i'm asking for attention when i doll up
i keep up with myself for me
i look good for me
i love me

"you can love yourself quietly"
i have
but i choose to allow my confidence and self love
to be loud and proud
my body, my choice

i am proud of my flaws and old insecurities
of course i will gracefully flaunt them
unapologetically too

i am not ashamed
so do not slut shame me for the confidence i wear

i don't seek your approval
i don't need your approval

let's talk about it

don't ever tell me "i'm asking for it"
because these thighs of mine
caught the eye of a man with a perverted, lustful mind

don't ever tell me "it's my fault" he was staring
because this bubble butt will move places
no matter what i am wearing

because rapists will always be attracted to you
you can be 3
you can be 42

i should not have to lower my appearance
just to not attract the attention from a rapist

it's your fault for blaming his actions
on one for having the same body parts as you

just as he is sexualizing my body, you are too

-you just exposed yourself

dear you

yes, i've been there before. i'm speaking to you. you feel as if you can't push anymore, as if you can't do it, as if you can't let go of the toxicity in your life. it's okay to not be okay. remember 6 months ago you got over that hard time?
you can do it again. remember that you lose yourself only to find a new and better you. you'll find more peace. you'll become peace. it's not overnight, but it will be worth seeing those pretty petals soon. hang on, rest.

-and if nobody told you today, you are strong and you've already come so far. don't give up.

to be continued...

i'm not done growing. i still have a lot more knowledge
to discover and absorb. i do know a lot, i have been through a lot
but not everything quite yet. through pain and struggle,
endurance is where growth comes from.

beauty in the struggle

i am from pain, i am from brokenness

you can't flourish without going through things

-come from it but don't be comfortable in it

priceless

my investment of my time and energy is expensive
yet something money can't and never will buy

silence

the wise do not bicker
with those who retain no knowledge

-don't become a fool arguing with the fool

FDT

if you think it's funny that donald trump
grabs women by their pussy

you too are the sexist and predator

sigh

using the r word as an insult is not okay. using someone's
disability as an insult or joke is not okay. just because you're not
saying it to somebody with a disability still doesn't make it okay.

*-they don't get it until they birth a mentally disabled child
or until its their loved one, then its "war over them."*

for the love of a daughter// demi lovato

i am here right in front of you

how are you here but you're dead?
shall i peel your skin to get to your mind?

i want to say come back
yet you're already far too gone

it's more than twice a month phone calls
with conversations that consist of silence

it's more than materialistic holidays

and now that i realize it
barbies and whatever i wanted bought my love
but it will never buy back the lost time

it will never buy the nights
you were partying, neglecting, abandoning
while your "angel from heaven" was in a place of darkness
crying herself to sleep because she was waiting for you
waiting for her superhero to save her

but sure, the money can buy you that addiction to take the edge
off
it can buy you those security cameras secured with your
delusions

and i thought you'd be the one to hold me
the one to wipe my tears
since the one you went half on a baby with

was supposed to nurture me and love me, didn't

i guess not
i guess you're the same person as her too

oh i can't imagine being a single dad
taking care of a babygirl on their own

wait did you even raise me?
was it you or your mom?

i wanna say yes
but you might claim the prize
look in the mirror though
mirror mirror on the wall
the man in the glass reflects it's a lie

they say a girl's first love is their father
yes, you were my first heartbreak

although there were many heartbreaks in my life after you
i looked for comfort from those that were just like you

you confused love and neglect
i thought a man in and out of my life was love
you confused how a man should love a woman
i thought a man who kept hurting me was love
you confused what effort actually was
i thought a man who fake tried was love
you made me think blood meant loyalty

anyways, do you hear me now?
are you still listening to what you wanna hear?
are you dead or am i even alive to you?

i used to wonder why i was always in the dark
i needed to see
i needed you

ameriKKKa

black and brown deaths
shouldn't be another statistic number
they're humans with families

there's anger in their grief
a mind going through war in silence
nightmares of regrets and wishes
endless rivers of tears in their prayers
endless running thoughts on "why?"
there's no "celebration of life" at funerals

only injustice

it's not that i don't care. i do, just not enough.

two cents

i stopped telling folks close to me about my ideas and goals
because they're usually the first ones to doubt.

LMAO

wanna know a funny joke?
amerikkka, twisted police, the government, the prejudice and the
privileged racists.

paths

if you want it, you'll make it work
don't grow apart, grow together

her to him

she said to him,
"i know you on your single shit but please don't lose sight"

inserts throwing up emoji

females in my town move so grimy
with grimy intentions

as to why i'm still out the mix
and forever will be out the mix

privacy

i think some forget i'm human at the end of the day, too.
besides business i'm very to myself and that's what i prefer.

i know i'm m.i.a. majority of the time.
i don't live for socials.

don't hit me up about what she said he said
don't ask me about people
don't update me on anything or anyone
don't ask where i've been
don't ask who i've been with
don't contact me just to be nosy
don't ask about my post, what i post is to be seen.

karma

the one you laugh at is the one who gets the last laugh.

i could tell when somebody has shit to lose by the grimy things
they openly brag about and publicly take pride in.

cause when you actually got shit to lose,
you move real different.

toll

once you get to the other side
and realize it can't even compare to mine,
do not come back to this side.

-it's a one way entry

me myself and i

i find that within my own company, i find myself more and more. there's nothing more beautiful than connecting deeper to your inner self.

-listen to her more

expectations

i don't go by time frame too much
i go by consistency

the more consistent i am
the closer i get to exceeding

void

i've changed
i've grown

you used to know me
you have to get to know me all over again
my old triggers are no longer part of me

you can't reach the old me
she no longer exists
your perception of the old me
is no longer valid

real love

if you love yourself unconditionally,
conditional love cannot hurt you
or phase you

wait

stop rushing God's plan, you haven't learned certain lessons yet.
if He blesses you before you learn the lesson and before you
retain the knowledge, you won't be able to sustain the blessing.
He'll change your mindset before He changes your situation.

-a lot of the time that's the problem. we try
to tweak it by forcing it now, when it's not where
He wants/needs us to be yet. don't step out
of season, there's a reason for every season.

his promise

his promise will come through
whether it's one month
or five years from now

it can take two years to get to that one year
that changes everything in life.

estate

you were my home

now what?

as heavenly as your name is
i felt hell on earth when we separated
and i've become restless

i think we both knew
we just didn't know when

we didn't know we wouldn't have
a last memory to hold onto with peace
only the memory of us walking away

i haven't healed yet obviously

it's why i write so much about you
about us
about what we were
the two we were supposed to be
past eternity

you planted hope in me
you planted raw in me
you planted life in me
you planted our home in me
full of you
full of vulnerability
but you took your seeds

and i'm dead inside
yet you're so alive

focus

when you don't look back
you're able to see the blessing
laying in front of you

i speak with intention and love
i speak from the soul
i speak truth

just because it's not what you speak
doesn't make my words invalid

shh.

the louder you get
the more quiet i become

you say, "why won't you respond?"
but i did

with wisdom
which is silence

v and h

there is nothing wrong with being vulnerable. allow
vulnerability and humility, those are the things that allow you to
feel. it's the confirmation to know you are alive.

who i am
everything i am

i'm not made for anything conditional

i love hard

so if you're not ready for unconditional love
please leave me alone

sometimes it's not others who hurt us
sometimes it's the lack of love we have for ourselves

-if we loved ourselves enough we would know
where to draw the line of what is okay and what is not.

grow up

inconsistency
lack of communication
dishonesty
conditional
nonchalantness

-how to lose a significant other
in ways besides cheating.

these days i'm solo
i've embraced this chapter

i'm now at ease
i gave my worries to God
i prefer my own company
i feel safer not letting the unknown in
it's not that i'm traumatized
i just know better now

pure peace

as i've gotten older
i appreciate my me-time more

no fake smiles
no forced conversations
no fake people

just myself
this pen
this paper

stepping stones

i outgrew you

where i'm going
not everybody can go

God said you can't come
so i'm leaving you where you're at
so i can meet Him where He needs me to be

posture

step into your inner self

are you aligned?

if not,
remove the things in the way of it

adjust like a chiropractor adjusts
the internal parts of you that need alignment

-our inner self is the foundation of our life.

clout vs. purpose

i don't do what i do or say what i say for "clout"

it's my purpose

forgive to release

i learned to forgive those who have trespassed against me.
the heavier my heart was, full of resentment, the deeper i was
under water. i had less room for God to come into my heart.

*-i forgive for my healing, not because i enable
or agree with one's wrong doings.*

sep 21 2019. sfo

as i sit in this airport i observe
how we all want to arrive
at the same destination

and that's how society is
everybody wants to do
what everybody is doing

it's the thing to do
it's called conformity

there's no purpose
just a bunch of roaming lost souls

it's not that i'm stuck
it's not that i'm holding onto you still

i'm holding onto the broken promises
the broken vows
the broken plans
the broken future

everything you promised me
and i held you accountable

you knew my past
you told me you would never

but you did

consciously
intentionally
consistently and constantly
with no hesitation
with no remorse

-so don't ask why i have trust issues.

i

your mindset mirrors your success
your success mirrors your mindset

more

if you want more
you have to be more

watch how that manifests

vs

this heart of mine
it's a blessing and a curse

it bleeds so much yet it's still full of honey

i can forgive somebody
who gives me every reason not to
so easily

it's always at war with my mind
with what i know

and my heart wins every time

mind vs. heart

the moment i start to act on faith and what i know instead of acting on my heart and feelings, is the moment many will question me.

i've realized there's so much beauty in simplicity.
i've realized how important your inner alignment, spirituality,
mindset and heart are, and how much they work together as
one.
i've realized how crucial it is to just let yourself free when your
feet hit the sea on the shoreline.
i've realized how beautiful it is to witness the sun and horizon
love again.

-the little things in life are the most important.
cherish it.

<3

better days
healed days

more life
more prosperity
more abundance
more blessings
more health
more wealth
more love
more peace
more clarity
more of me
more of God

ego. pride. thorns. knives.

we live in a world where pride is a normalized thing
like we rather wait till someone dies
or wait till time flies
to love

we live in a world
where ego is bigger than heart

we live in a world where staying silent
is equivalent to communicating emotions

we live in a world where time seems promised
like we're entitled to life

they're all one hell of a drug

the conformity of this society
it doesn't make sense
and for these reasons
the world we live in does not deserve me

*-never wait to love, there's no "right time."
only regrets on all the time wasted not showing
it when you should've, could've, and wanted to.*

reflection

does any of the stuff you've done and said,
reflect the love and loyalty
i have for you and given you?

let love flow freely
don't hold it in
don't hide in
don't try to make it go away

accept it
feel it
show it
love it

don't ask me why i don't reach out, come around or open up.
when each time i do you give me a reason to regret it.

it feels good knowing this current situation
is only temporary
knowing it gets better

sometimes you're the only bible people are going to read.

i refuse to give you the reaction and response you want to see out of me. sorry, my old triggers are no longer valid.

shattered men

why does my femininity intimidate toxic masculine men?

roots and blooms

love your roots just as much as you love your petals.

you can be the woman that God sent to him
be the woman who has everything they need and want

but if that man cannot see that
if that man cannot grasp it
it will never work

he will go through many seasons
of unnecessary waiting
just to realize you're the one

but don't wait on him
wait on God to fix him

some will only know you based off of other peoples opinions and words. some will only know you based off what you allow them to see. some will still only *want* to view you as the old you, instead of who you are today because they don't want to accept that you've changed for the better. everybody has their own version of you in their mind from their point of view. they can be one sided, which is just a reflection of their internal. which just exposes their level of understanding and how closed minded they truly are. don't take it personal. accept it and be at peace with it. you are not at an interview obligated to convince and prove if you've grown or not. you know you.

-stop playing with me and my growth.
their perception of you is not your responsibility.
your perception of me is not my responsibility.

nurturing the inners

as much as you take care of your physical, mental and emotional aspects of yourself, love your soul and spirit twice as much.

homebody

being out and being seen at every event is no longer my scene.
not because of my social anxiety, but i see no purpose in it,
literally my purpose doesn't align with that. i rather read a book
and educate myself with more knowledge, something that will
contribute to my legacy. i rather go to the beach and meditate in
peace, be in solitude in my own company, i rather be making
memories with loved ones. not that it makes me better, but i
choose to do other things. i'm over wasting time on things that
don't matter to me. which is okay.

comparable to none

i know there's many women out there that have bigger boobs,
bigger thighs, and a butt bigger than mine
but they will never be me

my heart, soul, mind, love
you cannot replace me

you will look for me in others

you will lust other females with hopes
of them being somewhat close to me

you won't find me

-humbly and respectfully.

too much or not meant?

i've learned that maybe it's not me

my love is just too much
all that i am is just too much
what i have to offer is just too much
it's all too pure, too true, too raw, too unconditional, too divine,
too rare, too overflowing.

some don't have the capacity to experience that.
but that's okay, that just means they weren't meant to.

*-now move, so you can make room
for those that will with no hesitation.*

bootlegs

they tell us to speak english because we're in america

yet when they travel to our countries
they suddenly love our culture
they suddenly know enough of our language

-just another country to mark off the bucket list, huh?
just another culture to absorb and mock
when you get back to america, huh?

living in a blue world

too many of our colored people dying
too many of our colored queens and kings crying
too many pleads of screams and "please"
too many singing the blues
caused by the ones wearing blue

the system serves no justice
just the privileged whites
cause they can't do no wrong
commit no crimes, right?
they get paid vacations on leave
and in the end the oppressed take time off
with no pay just to grieve

guns while he runs
guns while he prays
guns while god is the only witness
so when trial comes the case is dismissed

for the government everyday is the purge
defense is their favorite word
a non existent chapter in history books
something the kids have not heard
and will never learn

speaking up peacefully with a poster is a threat
remaining silently still with their hands up,
"don't shoot" will 99% lead to their death

speak and die
remain silent and die

walk and die
beg and die
comply and die

just die
the only thing we can do freely in a "free country"
in a nation full of hatred

there's no peace until the privileged reap what they sow
once it's their daughter, son, husband, wife or loved one
then it's no longer a joke

then they want the whole world to know
then they want their tears to matter
then they scream all lives matter

-what about the black and brown lives?

God's plan

ain't no plans b-z
when there is only
a plan
plan a
one plan
His plan

elevator

the more you elevate your mind
the more God will elevate your life

law

before you try to get that bag right
make sure you get that mind and spiritual right

                              -only way to sustain the blessings.

?

i noticed that the ones who criticize you most
or say the least
usually end up trying to copy your moves
and secretly take notes

weird, right?
but i guess weird people do weird things

the unhealed

hurt people hurt people.

-when you learn that how people treat you is a reflection
of their own internal war, you learn understanding and grace.
it's a reflection of their unhealed wounds, so hurting others
is the only thing they know to do since that's their
current state of mind and reality.

!!!

self care is so important. please don't forget to take care of yourself, too. you take care of your bills and errands first but it's time to take care of you first. you cannot pour into somebody else's cup when your cup is empty.

" "

the whole idea of "chasing a bag"
is so misunderstood

never chase the bag
never chase opportunities
never chase people

-i heard of the saying "maintain your energy so you can attract what aligns." which is so true because the more you are, the more you attract and the more your reality becomes. when you are aligned with your inner self you naturally just attract those good things in life. that's how you know it's meant for you too. pursue but do not chase. if you have to chase anything, that means it's running from you to begin with. shift your perspective. be it, attract it and pursue it.

i don't wear my money
i save to invest my money

it's in me, not on me.

-what God put in me is more important
than what i put on me.

one day

after so long when you least expected, it was just like that

one day...
she stopped posting about her feelings

one day...
she stopped replying to those texts
you sent her every now and then
she stopped answering those check up calls
just to see if you still had access to her

one day...
she stopped wishing and praying it would be you two again
she stopped holding onto something you easily let go of

one day...
she decided she didn't wan't to be broken,
waiting for nothing to happen anymore
so she stopped

she got up and started walking
on her journey to healing
on her journey to finding her worth
on her journey to be led to the man
God prepared her for

-i pray you find the strength to soon be her. God is with you, trust in
Him that he has better for you. you will feel empowered and whole
again. you are stronger than you think.

victim to victor

one day i woke up tired. i woke up tired of being tired. i wanted
more, i wanted different. i wanted the life i always dreamed of
and prayed for. i was tired of being victim. i wanted to become
victor of my struggles and past.

-the day you decide you no longer want to be victim
is the day you become victor.

commit to your vision. commit to your future. commit to the process. commit to being better, to being the best version of yourself. commit to what's right.

2good

in a world full of hustling and burning yourself out
nothing compares to God's favor

what man can do in 1 year
God can do in one moment

proverbs 18:21

manifestation and prayers are realer than real

there is power of life and death in your tongue
you can either bless yourself or curse yourself

-what's coming out of your mouth?
what's coming out of your circle's mouth?

you water the seeds you plant in your mind
what was once a thought becomes a reality in the physical

-be aware of what seeds you plant and what you water.
be aware of where you focus your energy.

the real criminals

there is a wall to keep my people out
to keep the "illegals" out

but what can we use to keep the privileged criminals out?
to keep them from doing illegal things to our communities?

*-what do we when the real criminals are our protectors
of the community, when they're part of our government,
when they're making decisions in the system?*

i speak up, i'm disrespectful
i remain silent and walk away, i'm childish
i distance myself, i'm toxic

-don't fall for toxic people's manipulative schemes
to get the reaction they want out of you,
just so they can guilt trip you in the end. remain firm.

vigilance

rejection is God's way of redirection and protection.

-he'll close a door to open five more. pay close attention to how he speaks to you and when he speaks to you. shift your perspective. be open.

perseverance

don't fold. keep going. when you feel done it means you're on
the verge of your breakthrough.

ily

love yourself. love yourself loud and proud. with no regrets. with no second thoughts. genuinely and thoroughly. confidently and unapologetically. love yourself first, always.

mental notes

i don't hold grudges, i just keep in mind who counted me out.

skyscraper

when you finally heal, please never meet people where they're at again. it's not being ignorant, it's setting boundaries for the sake of your peace and growth. stand and remain firm on your standards. never accommodate your worth. you have come too far to go back, to stay in place. you are deserving. you are worthy. their pain is not an excuse. understand the difference between being there for them in their season and lowing yourself.

-why would you pick your petals off
when the whole goal was to bloom?

she said to him

you don't care enough to try
you wouldn't care to leave

so i shouldn't care to walk away either
so you can't get mad or upset when i do

i don't match energy
i don't seek revenge
i don't go out of my way
i don't stoop down to levels

i accept it, remove myself, pray about it, and level up

i just want to be around good energy
energy that will elevate me
and make me better in every aspect

to be a woman is so much more beautiful
than people actually realize

who we are
what we can do
what we can create

we met in 2015 at the el camino vs. south city bell game. i was a cheerleader at the time. my cousin who is also your best friend brought you and we were introduced to each other. i never believed in love until you. i was 15 you were 16. i had this weird feeling about you, i genuinely felt like i've known you in another lifetime. your energy. from there it was history. i was hurt at the time. as time went on you taught me how to love, how to accept love and show it. our story is ours. our love is ours. i know our love is past eternal. nobody will compare to us. i love to love you. i love your love. thank you for all the memories. thank you for all the face kisses and tight hugs when i'm upset. thank you for the wisdom. thank you for loving me at my worst. we've grown so much. i've learned things about you that has made me adore you more and more. we're not perfect, but worth it. thank you for being the person you are and for loving me even when i couldn't/didn't love me. our journey has been imperfectly beautiful. my bestest friend, i thank god for you. thank you for it all.

promises// jhene aiko

09/12/15. amerie love, my baby love. my greatest blessing. when you were born you changed my whole life. your birth was the birth of something that would change both of our lives forever. we're 15 years apart but our hearts couldn't be closer in love. i will always be your protector, your ateh, your superhero, your right-hand. everything i do is for you, and when you read this as you get older i pray you hold it closely to you. i know i had to leave but one day you'll understand. i just want to give you everything i never had, and to create a legacy for you to take on. i love your kisses and hugs, your laugh is so pure. your eyes that are so sparkly. you amaze me daily. my love for you is unconditional and i thank god for you. i will forever be your keeper.

good peeps

its something about having a good heart
about having a forgiving heart
we can never seem to get it right
to leave after we've been stabbed with a knife
or is it them that can't get it right to do us right?

it's something about giving people the benefit of the doubt
even though they've shown their true colors
even though they know what they did

they say we're "too nice"
but if i stopped being the loving and forgiving person i am
and brought the old me out,
they'd say i'm cold for cutting them off
they'd say i'm toxic and petty for matching their energy
cause that's exactly what the old me would've done
after the first time they hurt me

can the good hearted ever win?
you be the bigger person, you get stepped on
you finally stop allowing things
you finally set boundaries
you're the bad guy and now they're victim

it will always hurt you to stay
just as much as it will hurt you to walk away from them

i mean, i rather be too loving and too forgiving than not at all
i would hate to live in resentment and hatred

     -never stop being a good, loving, forgiving person–
just stop being a good, loving, forgiving person to the wrong people."

time and plan

sometimes we forget that God's timing and his plan must be in correlation. we can't just accept his plan for us then expect it to happen tomorrow morning. we have to accept his plan and also accept his timing. we can't just accept his timing for us then try to alter his plan. we can't just accept his plan for us then try to alter his timing.

-you never know who and what He's saving us from just by making us wait longer or moving us faster, just by changing our plan.

from me to me

it wasn't your fault. the environment you were in was just too toxic. you had no control over what happened, over who said what and who did what. you tried your best. you tried to protect the best way you knew how. i know you didn't understand. you were so lost. you were so confused. you were so alone. you were so dead inside. you were so full of fear. i remember. you're in a better place now, you're free now. you've grown. you've healed. you've learned. you are new. you found god. you found your calling. you are so full of love, so full of wisdom, so full of forgiveness, so full of strength. don't be ashamed, be proud of your old hurt. it is your testimony. wear it loud and proud. tell the world like you mean it. it will help heal others who were once the old you. you broke so many generational curses without even knowing. it didn't make sense then but i bet it does now. you didn't fail, you didn't go back, you didn't fold. don't forget who you are, don't forget what made you and where you've come from. never forget there's true beauty in the struggle. you are the rose that arose from the concrete. i admire everything you've been through. look at you now, you made it. you're doing it big and better. own it.

-who i was back then needed
the woman i am today. i love me.

sometimes it takes two to heal so two can love
so two can grow into 1

how can we love if we don't love ourselves first?
how can we fill each other's cup if we're both empty?

we don't even have a life jacket to save one another from
drowning in the middle of the sea of our love and promises

sometimes it'll take time to get things right
sometimes it'll take time to realize

but isn't it crazy how we can be so empty
yet so whole when we're together?
how we can be so lost yet found when we're both around?
how we can be so broken yet healed when we're both here?

as much as i need me most
as much as you need you most

it's as if we need each other more

i'm never asking for too much
what i ask for will never be too much either

anything i ask of or require from one,
i'm able to reciprocate 10x more with no hesitation

healing

you must release to receive. imagine this:

i am holding all these groceries and physical items in my hands. i
can't grab anything else until i put them down and let go of it. i
can barely move because of how heavy it is. i can't even take
another step. it's painful, my hands are hurting.

those groceries and physical items represent everything negative
i'm holding onto, that is holding me back from moving forward.
that is literally weighing me down. those groceries and physical
items represent hatred, resentment, pain, my past, jealousy,
entitlement, etc. you say you want God to give you better and
come into your heart to heal you, yet look; there's no more
room for Him! how can you receive those blessings when your
hands and heart are full of those things?

the enemy wants you to stay bonded, he wants you to be
weighed down, he wants you to be stuck, he doesn't want you to
have room for God. he doesn't want you to receive those
blessings.

put the bag down. release those things so you can receive what
God is trying to give you.

she said

she said, "when i'm silent
it means i'm done in every aspect
it means i'm drained mentally, emotionally, spiritually
it means i don't have anything left in me to say
nothing left in me to give
it means i'm tired of being tired
i'm over it
it means i am dead inside
that's how you know i'm no longer here

it means you're about to miss the me who was "trippin"
for seeing what i saw
who was "insecure" for body wounds from the battlefield made
of your lies
who was "crazy" for being right
who was "too clingy" for just trying to love you
who was "too sensitive" for hurting from the pain you've caused
who was "too deep" for expressing my feelings
who was "too much" for wanting your love

you should've heard me while you were able to
while i still spoke
while i still cared to try

when i'm silent is the only time you should fear all of my love
cause it may no longer be here anymore
cause now that i've reached this point after so many times of
trying
after so many times of questioning myself
there's no going back to the loving, forgiving me
i'll never be the same
        no matter if you ever change"

her decisions

she said, "i'm not difficult– i just have standards that i require.
due to that, i've decided i no longer want to be in a situationship.
i've decided i don't want to be committed to an uncommitted
relationship. i am no longer fond of being the glue that tries to
hold our broken foundation together just to add one more
wrong on top of it while you witness it crash on me. i don't want
to be the hidden gem under a rock anymore cause you're
paranoid of us being in sight. i don't want to be 'a season of
love.' i don't want my words or feelings to come off as if i'm
complaining. i don't want to compare myself to other females
who're "your type" anymore. i don't want to count all of my
reoccurring trust issues and insecurities that you've created. i
don't want to be a collection that collects dust. i don't want to be
a thought you try to not think about. i want the same
consistency and effort you put into seeking the waters.
i want the same love you give out to everyone that were never
there for you who has never even seen you cry, who has never
even wiped your tears. i want you to love me with no hesitation,
the same way you never hesitated to do what you did. i want to
be the answer to your prayer, the one you prayed for. i want to
be chosen everyday
even if everyday isn't always sunflowers and sunlight. i want you
to look at me and know there's only 1 of me. though you keep
me around cause you don't want to see me loving another how i
tried to love you, cause you don't want to see another loving me
how i ask you to. but why? if you know you can't, won't, and
don't want to, why do you continue to hang onto me? while
you're thinking of what to say back, i've decided."

trees in the water

while i tried to help you grow
while i tried to build you up, you elevated
i sunk

they say what doesn't kill you makes you stronger
but it seems like i died inside because of all the pain
it seems like it killed me more and more
every time i tried to get back up
you continuously broke me down

the second i got back up
you'd knock me right back down

i am wounded
i have permanent scars
i was trying to put the pieces of myself
that you shattered
back together

my own love wasn't even anywhere close enough to heal me
it would take only God's miracle to mend, revive and heal
what seemed to be too dead and broken

shoulda coulda woulda

i should've stayed ready for this
i mean, i knew it was going to happen again
i guess it was just a matter of when
i should've never let my guard down again
i should've kept it up
i should've listened to my intuition
i thought maybe this time it would be different for the better
i should've known better

this time will be the last time
this time i'll use this as my fuel
to never go back to what broke me in the first place
this time i know there's no healing there

-even though part of me knew, a bigger part
of me wanted you to prove me wrong.

to do list

free yourself
nurture yourself
love yourself
elevate yourself
ground yourself

the blue sky and hills

i'm watching the birds play together
i'm watching them fall in love

look at the hills
how they stand tall, connected together
how they hold space for each other
they are alive and watching
they are each other's puzzle piece
they can kiss the boundless blue sky
the hills can feel the sun's warmth
so imperfectly perfect
so imperfectly aligned

life is so beautiful even in bad seasons
there is so much beauty in simplicity

this is god's work in the simplest form

i just want to reassure you that you are loved. you deserve to heal. you deserve a love that won't perish in the hardest seasons to love you. you deserve to genuinely smile. you deserve to sleep free of pain and fears. you are worthy. God sees you, He feels your pain, He's working even when you don't see it or feel it. I declare victory over the battle you're facing, peace over the war in you mind, and healing over the wounds in your heart. i know your healing feels uncomfortable but that just means you're growing. it's not easy. it doesn't feel good at all. but still choose it. the future you needs you to release. you are bigger than what hurt you. the scars you have indicate how far you have come.

please don't give up.

i had to learn the difference between having a good, loving, forgiving heart and allowing someone's pain as an excuse to continuously hurt me.

-never confuse the two ever again.

say out loud,

"today is the day i choose to no longer go through that toxic situation. i choose to no longer give it my time or energy."

-keep repeating. speak it till you believe it.
believe it, speak it, claim it.

when you heal, you don't just heal for you.
you heal for your future kids and future grandchildren.
you break generational curses.

just because that person wasn't able to love you the way you deserve, don't allow that to determine your worth.

you are so worthy and deserving. if he/she can't after trying so much that just means they were never meant to. that means God has somebody better for you.

please don't let society define you.
know who you are in God.
i know it's hard to recognize yourself sometimes
but love you are so divine inside and out.
you may not feel like it right now,
though you will soon.
i promise.

you're bigger than the person who hurt you
you're bigger than the person who left you
you're bigger than the person who filled your ears
with broken promises

what they did to you isn't because of anything you did
but simply because of the internal war they're facing.
once you understand that you won't take it as personal

how can i be your peace of mind
when you've caused hell on earth between us?

i think my brokenness led me to a point in my life where i realized it wasn't me losing my faith. i never lost faith, i lost myself.

trauma normalized

don't you wonder why it feels a lot easier
to hold the weight of the pain on your shoulders
than it is to walk freely?

it seems as if sitting in our puddle of tears
is like a warm and comforting jacuzzi numbing our pain away

1 thing about me
i'm extremely loving and forgiving

though once i stand firm on being done
9/10 you'll never witness that side of me again

not due to me putting any walls up
or being prideful with resentment
but because i choose boundaries for the sake of my peace

don't hurt the woman God sent to you to help heal you.

-she's just fulfilling God's work that you requested,
He was answering your prayer through her.

be careful what you wish for

if we don't speak anymore cause of you and your choice to not
talk, then there's no way i'll ever reach out. not cause of pride
and ego, only cause i'm doing my part by standing firm and
respecting your decision.

sometimes forgiving somebody may feel like swallowing thorns.
it's one of the things that will set you free.

-choose it, even if it hurts.

serpents

deception comes in all forms that are closest to the treasures and
desires of your heart. don't lose sight. stay focused.

blessing in disguise

i got tired of the switch ups
but i was so thankful for the true colors

i'm big on unconditional love
i'm heavy on loving
i'm heavy on loyalty
i'm heavy on all my standards
especially my worth

all gas no brakes

i hope that when you heal from those wounds
you use that fuel as power towards tunnel vision
to create a better you

i haven't been in the mix since i was 15,
you'll see me when you see me.

beauty is pain

every time i see butterflies, it makes me reminisce.

it makes me remember they will shortly
turn into poisoned butterflies
dropping like my heart into the pit of my stomach.

every time i see beaches it reminds me of all the times
i was drowning in my own sea of love
waiting for you to rescue me
like you said you would.

every time i see rain falling from the skies
it reminds me how much the angels cried
when you said "goodbye bye for now"
knowing it was actually your last

you sucked the beauty out of beauty
you turned it from being so breathtaking
to taking my breath away till i die

you turned the little things
into the biggest living nightmares and painful triggers

turned something so sweet into something so bitter
it makes you wish you would've known better

stop apologizing for being you

when you reach a level of growth
when you are truly authentic
unapologetically you
and stand on your worth

those who are stagnant
those who aren't authentic
those who are weak minded
and those who don't know their worth
will always be intimidated by you

wow.

it sucks seeing the person you took so much time on
to build and help heal
give the love you wanted, give the love you gave
to another so easily, so freely, so painlessly with no hesitation

i told you once i felt like i was building you
for the next but damn i didn't think you'd agree

sucks that the next gets to experience
the reaping of what i sowed into you

and in the end
i look like i'm the one holding a grudge
i look like the one who's petty

when really i'm just disappointed i spent so much time waiting

when really i'm just disappointed
that you made me believe we could be something great
after your "season of healing those wounds"
that you said was the reason you couldn't love me or value me

was it that or were your eyes somewhere else the whole time?
or did you just lose sight in the process?

you said i'd always know where your heart is
but clearly i don't cause it's no longer with me
cause clearly you're out of reach

all i have left is music telling me
i should've known better, that i'll eventually be okay

all i have left is people from church telling me they'll pray

but fuck that
i gave you more than i ever gave myself
when i thought there was no more in me to give
there goes something that i always ended up giving you
there was no such thing as giving you my last
cause my love and forgiveness for you never ran out

but i think i'm finally putting a stop to that

you got to experience my overflow of abundant love
just to take it with you and leave to give to somebody else
and now you're telling me i gotta sit and be okay with this?
like you didn't plant a home in me, like it ain't that deep?

now i got no choice but to move on like it's nothing
as if we weren't more than something the naked eye can see

i guess that was the one promise you never broke
that if it wasn't me
i said i want you to appreciate and value the next
so they never sit in regret and question if they're worthy enough
so they don't have to say the words coming out my mouth
or feel what i feel

i know some days seem worse more than they are better. but understand flowers can only bloom when rain falls. you're coming out. you are reaping what you've sown.

i'd rather stumble taking steps
than remain complacent not taking steps

as the days go by
i've come to the conclusion
i'm okay with being alone

i'm okay with being the only one who loves me
who appreciates all that i am
all that i give

your absence taught me how to be content
without you

i'd rather be alone and whole
than taken and hurt

it feels good to choose me again
it feels good to finally realize and fully believe
i don't deserve anything less than what i give

i'm okay.

-to be alone is not lonely, to be alone is
to recharge. be okay with it.

healing happens when you decide you no longer want to be victim, when you decide you're no longer going to allow your trauma and wounds to dictate your daily life. healing happens when you hand over your control to God.

i used to get upset when people didn't get my vision
or when people had negative things to say about my vision

i used to get upset when people didn't clap for my
accomplishments especially if they knew what it took to
accomplish that goal

but then i realized it just means they were never meant to get it
that just means the right audience and people will find me

-some become envious because it's hard for them
to accept the fact you both come from the same place
and you're the one who elevated.

you did all you can love. you tried with all of you. you gave all of you. you prayed the deepest prayers. there was nothing you could've done to make him stay. let him leave. let him be with the one he left you for so he can realize he messed up. so he can realize it doesn't get any better than you, that no woman will ever love him the way you did. don't beg when there's a man praying for the godly and spiritual woman you are. either he will see in due time, or in due time he will see another man who loves you with 0 hesitation. why do you want to be with somebody who doesn't want you? prepare to heal instead. prepare to forgive. prepare to let go of what left you so easily. you are so deserving and so worthy.

don't let one's blindness and ability to see your worth ruin your opportunity to finally receive the love you give and deserve.

self-awareness

you can 100% be politically correct, yet 110% emotionally
wrong.
how you approach matters. how you communicate matters.

hush

sometimes the world and chaos can be too loud to hear God, literally. be still. delete the apps. turn the music off. turn the tv off. shut the outside noise off and be silent to hear Him speak.

-when you become still and vigilant,
you will hear all the voicemails and see all
those unread messages and calls from God.

you gain wisdom and strength from pain, not comfortability.

when you shift your perspective, you turn that thing that was
once pain, into purpose.

no, i'm good

i don't want to be in the presence of somebody
who doesn't fear my absence
who is too nonchalant
when reconciliation is too hard to imagine

it's not a grudge
it's not daddy issues
it's not that i didn't forgive

i just know better now
to never let you in again
to never give you the opportunity
to hurt me again
to never give you me

cause now i'm left damaged,
too damaged for the right one who comes around
and i might potentially damage him
from the pain you've caused
from the love i lost

i'm too scared to let another in
who knows if they're actually good
i'm too scared to find out it's the same shit
to only be reminded of what love isn't

so like i said, i'm good
i don't want a love that's conditional or fictional
when mine is more than sustainable
when the love i have is written in the books of scripture

if you don't have the intention to do me right
please don't even bother
i'm too good for what you have to offer
i don't need to reap any more pain that was sowed into me
or live through another traumatizing chapter
when i barely survived the last back to back episodes

i'm too solid for anything less than what i give
so if that means being alone and living without you,
then so be it

life is a healing journey

i realized in every season you'll always be healing from
something
you just become stronger
you just gain more knowledge to help you through

which is why i believe there's no wrong or right time to love

it's not that things got too difficult between you two because
of the season, you just have to be with somebody who is willing
to love you in every season no matter how stormy it gets.

*-side note: God also says find peace in Him in the storm,
find Him and you'll find peace. things get better but they
don't get easier you just become stronger.*

i'm turning the page on what we tried to write
on what we tried to create
on what we were supposed to be
our book of promises

the picture is beautiful
just how we could've been

but this time i'm turning the page
and letting God rewrite the story

don't fall for the calls or texts when he checks up on you.
he knew exactly what he was doing. understand there was
nothing impulsive about his action(s), lust begins in the mind
before it manifests into the physical world.

walks and costs

walking with God isn't free

it costs you some people you've been around for years
who're the only people you know
it costs you those habits that seem like the right way to live life
it costs you some time in solitude
it costs you that wall you took years to build
it costs you leaving everything behind without turning back

but whatever you lose during that walk with God
He replaces with better
with the ordained
with the things and ones meant for you

*-it costs but what you get from it is priceless and
everlasting. you'll never lose, you only receiver better.*

don't let other people's lack of faith kill your faith.
don't let their lack of relationship with God
determine how you view Him.

i've always been looked at as the girl in the family who didn't have parents, who went through a lot, who had a hard life. i've always been the girl everybody felt sorry for.

for once i just want my struggles to be viewed as my testimonies, as the woman with the story God wrote for her. i want to be viewed as an unbreakable woman, with pure wisdom. of course i'm proud of how far i've come but let's switch the perspective. i don't want people in my presence only because they feel bad knowing i was once neglected cause of the absence. i don't want people having my number only because they feel bad knowing i'm currently not in contact with my parents. be around me and contact me because you truly want to.

i remember

i remember those visits with the mediator at four
i remember having my first lawyer at six
i remember lying to authorities out of fear
i remember being forced to lie
i remember having to skip recess because the cps social worker
needed to speak to me
i remember being scared to speak
i remember being scared to tell the truth i had to write my
response on a white board
i remember calling cps to make the report myself at eight
i remember asking myself if i'd ever know what it's like to have a
family
i remember all the police departments in different cities
i remember all the police standbys from parent to parent
i remember all the neglect, trauma and broken promises
i remember all the verbal, mental and emotional abuse
i remember making observations on everyone around me at
school, i always wondered why they had parents and a better life
i remember the first time i tried killing myself wanting to die,
it turned into a constant thing and i didn't even hit puberty yet
i remember the first time i saw blood leaking down my arm from
the knife, crying and smiling cause it was bittersweet
i remember all those nights crying myself to sleep
i remember every single one of my sixteen therapists
i remember every single school counselor
i remember all the fears
i remember having to do life alone
i remember begging my dad to not let me go back to my moms,
even though i knew he was just gonna leave to party by night
time
i remember every place and city i've lived in,

there was no such thing as home
i remember telling myself in the mirror it's survival mode or die
at nine
i remember the absence and toxic presence
i remember sleeping with knives and pepper pray under my
pillow
i remember holding amerie while praying to God to keep us safe,
to let us make it through another night, just one more at least
i remember asking God if this would be my/our last night alive
i remember how tired i was from everything,
realizing this was my life and that i couldn't change it at fifteen
i remember wondering if i'd ever see light again knowing i never
knew what light was to begin with
i remember finding out the one who made me only had
intentions on killing me
i remember it all

*-this isn't even close to everything i remember. i don't spill this to be felt
sorry for. if you don't plan on raising your children, being there for
them or loving them, simply do not have them. this is a lifetime
commitment, not when you feel like it. we remember everything. we feel
everything. it traumatizes us and molds our future relationships. some
heal and grow from it, some don't and never will. i am blessed to have
the strength and courage to speak on it but not everybody will so please
be conscious.*

i love how much we connect
our energy proves there's no such thing as time or distance

i love how you know exactly what to say when i can't think
the yin to my yang

i can't imagine life without you
i don't want to imagine it either

past eternal is ours, love is ours to keep

u and i

i know we're meant
your love says it all

there's no denial
everyone knows

even on bad terms
it's never out of sight

with you i can never lose
you just remind me how blessed i am
to at least have you

when the world is on my shoulders
you take it off

when you see tears on my face
you wipe them before they fully fall

when life throws me off
you keep me grounded

when i need reassurance you remind me
your love is always boundless

these days i can no longer compromise
it costs too much

i can no longer meet others where they're at
i've overcome too much
i've come too far just to go back

i can't compromise my worth anymore
i'll no longer apologize for it either

my gama's strength will always amaze me.

she carried the weight of the world on her shoulders
while trying to raise 3 kids in that same cold world

her love remained unconditional even when her lover
broke her down and tried to kill her

she gave us her last and said as long as we're happy and fed,
she's blessed

she made ends meet even when the distance seemed unreachable

she kept every promise even when everyone around her folded

she was the backbone when there was no foundation to keep us
up when she was the one crumbling

she prayed to God about us before praying for herself

God sent her to be our answered prayer

there's nothing that could amount to everything she has done for
me and my loved ones. she is a heaven-sent angel in human
form. a pure blessing. a legacy to be forever kept.

regrets and cake

so many people have always me asked what i regret in life.
my answer is alway nothing.
i would've never found my purpose, i would've never found God,
i wouldn't be who i am today.
the recipe matters.
anything i regret and didn't go through would mess up today's
outcome.
the most painful stories that are the easiest to regret, were the
most important parts.
it's what makes you so unique.

*-the main ingredient to cake is flour. if i didn't use flour there would be
no cake. it would't become what it's known for. flour is extremely messy
too. even the messiest parts of our lives is the thing that makes our
outcome most beautiful. never regret any pain. it was needed. it was
110% mandatory. now you can tell others how you made your cake.
pass the recipe down sis, there's others struggling to make the cake too.*

l o v e

as scary as love may seem
it's so beautiful with the right person

it's easy to push love away
when you've been hurt so many times

but don't give up
God was just preparing you for the right one
He was preparing the right one for you, too

victory

God was by my side the whole time
i was never lonely
these scars are my testimonies
they indicate my courage of getting up and never giving up

He heard my cries
He felt my pain
He doesn't play about his children
so now every person who ever did me wrong
and watched me fall
has no choice but to witness the table
that He had prepared for me after all

even when it seemed like moving my feet became deadly,
those battles were the very things getting me ready
for the blessings and the praise
for my present better days

i wish i knew God at an earlier age.

i knew of Him because my filipino family was religious but i never actually knew Him. i knew He was a God of miracles but i didn't know He was for me. if i knew Him when i was younger maybe i wouldn't have felt so lost and afraid. He would've been my comfort. i would've depended on Him instead of depending on my fight-or-flight-self. maybe i would've been at peace knowing He was in control.

best by: _/_/_

old foes and faces
i witnessed them fold

it got old
nowadays i just wanna grow

which means i gotta leave

sorry if you can't get ahold of me
you'll see me when you see me

i can still forgive you and not want reconciliation
i can still love you from a distance

it's no hate
i guess you can say it's the weather these days
just not feelin it like i used to
i'm ready for something healthy and new

harsh check:

are you healing or are you distracting yourself to fill the void to make it seem like you're healing when you're really not? are you distracting yourself with the things that led you to the destruction you now have no choice but to heal from?

be

be the woman who is courageous
who is unapologetically herself in a crowd of masks
who stands firm on her worth
who knows when to leave a harmful situation
who knows how to love herself when the world doesn't
who isn't afraid to speak loud when the room is silent

be the woman God has called you to be

be her and love her
be proud of her

-step into that real you, she is waiting for you.
and please understand it's okay if you can't
be her just quite yet, grow to be.

i am grateful for all the lessons.
i didn't live through it just for me,
i now get to tell my future kids and future generations.

i can now prevent the hurt
i can now help heal the hurt
i can now share the wisdom they were searching for
i can now introduce them to the miracle worker
i can now leave a legacy that is everlasting

,

please don't hurt me

i've been wounded too much
i'm too familiar with the pain

don't get mad at my trust issues
or insecurities
i didn't ask for them
i'm still trying to get rid of them
it feels like resurfacing wounds that just won't close

yes, i need constant reassurance
i'm clingy only because i know a good thing

my past was ugly
but i promise who i am today is so worth it

just be gentle with me
i'm very fragile
but i promise my love is strong enough to keep us together

sometimes God may be working through you to answer
somebody's prayer and you may not even realize it. He may be
using that person to answer your prayer too. don't question it.
your discernment will never lie. the Holy Spirit is 110%
accurate.

blooming blessings

sometimes your blessings are like a flower. it is planted, but not
yet ready to bloom. sometimes God is still working on you.
you're not ready to be seen. if you bloom too early, you may not
be able to sustain the season.

still seasons

a lot us may know what it's like to grind for it. but do you know what it's like to pray and wait for it? to not step out of season cause of impatience?

some blessings are all about waiting in a season for it to come to pass. there is nothing man can do to hurry it up no matter how much you grind. it's a season of being still, of your faith being tested in a season of silence.

-still praise in advance.

i prefer my peace over attention.
everybody can contact me,
but not just anybody has access to me.

-understand the difference.

it sucks being the one who's always misunderstood when i'm so understanding.

3 am thoughts

the truth is, i just wanna be where you are. i just wanna grow with you. i just wanna love you till my love overflows.

milestone appreciation

as i'm transitioning into my 20's i've never appreciated my time more than now. i appreciate the present. more love, simplicity, gratitude, humility, vulnerability. nothing less, only that or better. life is so much more beautiful than it seems. sometimes i think i feel too much but it just reminds me that's how i know i'm alive and living.

she walks this earth with purpose
she is capable of anything

her touch is pure
her voice is soft but just as reckless
as the waves of the sea when firm
her body is her temple but she lets her guard down for this one
man
she is comfortable by herself so her presence is a privilege

she is made with spiritual gifts
she is magic

i don't know where to start
but i guess i'll say this from my heart

i gotta stop wearing it on my sleeve
cause anytime i open up it's devoured

fool me once it's whatever
fool me again shame on me

it's just hard cause my love is made of things better than gold
it really just ain't in me to ever fold

do you hurt me or am i hurting myself?

i guess we are different
i guess that's why we just had to call it quits

s.s.f.

nights of fear
nights of cries
nights of sleeping with knives

nights of wishing i should've ran away when i could
and find love somewhere else for good

hoping the night skies would love me
and maybe tell me everything will be alright

hoping the cold winds would guide me on my path
hoping the boundless cities would help me
just a lost child seeking everything they lacked

she called him and said,

"God applied some pressure and you folded
you chose them over me

you promised you would never
but broke those promises so easily

you said we'd make it work no matter the situation
then you dipped and here i am still trying to forgive

i know i'm not perfect
but damn this doesn't even amount"

new beginnings or maybes

i just wanna get away
be so far away that i start over

i wanna see a different sky
feel different air
experience a different culture

i'm taken advantage of
i'm never heard
what i give is never reciprocated
i'm too much

maybe my love is the miracle water to the plants and trees
maybe that new world will love me deeper than flesh
maybe that new world will hug me so tight
maybe that new world will reciprocate everything i give and
more
maybe it will hear my voice when i speak
maybe i was that one missing piece that was never too much
i was the missing puzzle piece all along
maybe i'm the answered prayer to that new world
or maybe that new world is the answer to my prayer

maybe i should remain silent and never speak again
maybe i should remain still and never love again
maybe i should leave and never come back

maybe i'd be enough then
maybe i'd matter then

i will never be ashamed to tell my story, to tell others where i've come from and the things i got through. these scars are now testimonies to help others heal. there's no secret, there's no price. call me an open book but this is my purpose. embrace your past. embrace every season.

daddy issues

it's the conditional love from our conditional fathers on earth
that mold our view on relationships
they are the first ones to break our hearts
the first ones to leave us
the first ones to promise things that never happen
the first to be inconsistent in our lives
they're the reason we walk with our heart guarded when we step
out into the world that they warned us about
they're the first reason we don't trust

and majority of women with fathers like these, naturally go after
men that are similar to our conditional fathers to fill the hole
they created and left, labeling your man as the one man you
could finally trust—with the hopes of him being different than
the type of men you are used to. aka your conditional father.

isn't it crazy how there are men that women date that do what
they did, yet aren't fathers?
These conditional fathers are just conditional men, take away
"father" in "conditional father," and all you're left with is
"conditional."

> -please stop thinking that just because you're not a man with a
> kid, doesn't give women the ability to compare you to or label you as
> "just like my dad."

sometimes it's necessary to go completely m.i.a.

the healer needs healing too

she cried saying

"i don't wanna love again. i don't wanna open up anymore. i don't believe in forever anymore. i don't even recognize who i am when i look in the mirror anymore. i never thought i could feel so ugly or develop so much self-hatred. my mind keeps running and all those women keep popping up in my head. i'm going crazy, i've lost my sanity. i've witnessed too much, i've been through too much, i've been hurt too much, lied to too much to even think there is someone who will stand on every word despite the seasons. i don't wanna feel like the ugliest thing on earth again. i don't want to beg for love again. i don't want to fight for a position in someone's life just for them to choose me as their last resort if their original plan doesn't work again. i don't want to feel like i have to watch somebody again. once was enough. once killed me several times. the one person i ever trusted, loved, confided in and made promises with turned around on me like it was nothing. so i guess you can say i'm still broken. i'm still trying to pick up the pieces shattered by you. i guess you can say i have major trust issues. i guess you can say i'm drained and tired. i guess you can at this point i don't expect anything good but pain. i guess you can say i've turned numb."

-i pray no more females go through this again. it will be okay love. this is just temporary, you'll be happy again. you are beautiful and amazing. don't let a man convince you otherwise due to his blindness.

it doesn't matter how healthy or good your communication is. if
one doesn't have the ability to comprehend, don't even waste
your breathe trying to explain your point. don't get frustrated.
don't let your emotions win. don't be impulsive. pray for their
understanding and walk away peacefully.

i know that i am destined
i know that ahead are so many blessings

meant for me
calling my name
waiting for me to say, "i am ready for you"
for everything that is ordained

only prosperity
abundance
and peace
there's nothing more that i seek

patient
open
called
proven by abraham and his promised land
this is God's plan

i was born into an environment i was supposed to repeat
i was supposed to live in the cycle i come from

where drugs and toxic abuse is the norm
where the devil has his foot on

but i've been chosen to break it
to never repeat
to only defeat

i'm at a place in my life where i choose my peace of mind and
sanity over trying to get my point across.

all these petty fights
you say you got the right

you said it ain't pain to you,
yeah cause it didn't happen to you

but we both know if i did you how you did me
you would hate my guts

feelings change
things change
life moves at a fast pace
i just never thought it would've changed your endurance

why promise things you knew you couldn't live up to?
now i hold you accountable for all the pain i'm going through

or maybe it's my entitlement to your loyalty and love
or maybe it was the pride feeding your ego

you said this would be best for us
as if i'm not best for you
as if you and i aren't better together

you got me on your side while you look out into the world
and you still haven't learned that the world doesn't love you
back,
never more than i have and ever will

the more i heal the more you resent me.

i never got closure whenever i left a place i thought was home
city to city
new faces
old faces
and i still felt alone

advice on life
being told the life i lived was never even right

it was never okay
no amount of apologies with affection could take this pain away
yet i'm so numb

there's no one to blame since that was all my parents knew
or should they have known better?

daily affirmation

i am aligned and well.
i am aligned and well.
i am aligned and well.
i am aligned and well.
i am aligned and well.

pain turns into blessings that were already ordained.

circle aka distraction

"friends" don't influence and contribute to your bad habits,
especially the devil's way.

she left him a voicemail

"was the lust and temptation worth what God had for us?
was the moment satisfying enough?

you know they'll never be me and you hate it
that's why you get uncomfortable anytime i say it

you smoke the pain away
distract the pain away
meet every chick you follow on the gram

but love, you're losing yourself trying to find me in them"

so many territories colonized
just to be claimed as a 1st founder prize

how can you be founder
when its been founded before you were even alive?

i'm souled out.

i am soul searching, i'm unraveling the precious things about myself i never knew of. i am on the way to meeting the best me.

why're you the resentful one when you're the one who quit on us?

finally, she started to bloom
the rain and clouds turned into blue skies filled with butterflies
what were once roots blossomed into petals
her mind elevated to a different level

she was able to see the rainbow
and see the sun that made her aura glow

there was love
there was gratitude
there was light

this was finally her time

from me to you

to the reader,

i pray you find comfort and healing in my words that i've written. i don't know what you've been through and i don't know you're current storm. but i do know that despite your past and present, you are more than worthy and deserving. you deserve to heal, grow, you deserve happiness, love, and everything that God has for you. never question it. don't let your hurt and other people's opinions define your amazing worth. God made you with intention and purpose. life is hard but you become stronger. don't ever give up. keep going and growing. never stop loving. never stop forgiving. the storm will pass.